A Bundle of Sticks

An Aesop Fable

Retold by Elena Martin
Illustrated by Diana Kizlauskas

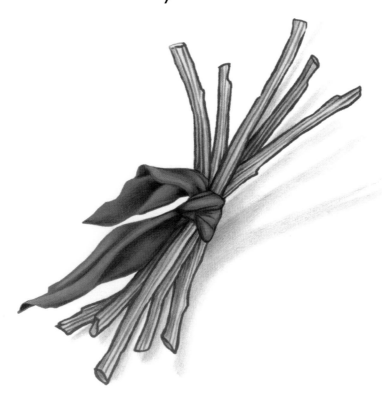

Rigby

A Harcourt Achieve Imprint

www.Rigby.com
1-800-531-5015

Once there was a wise king named Dalmar. The king had five sons. The sons were always fighting. They never agreed on anything!

The princes argued all day long.
Each one believed he was the best.
Each of them wanted to have the best
of everything. None of them wanted
to share or work together. That was a
big problem.

At breakfast Prince Kofi wanted everyone's attention. "Look at this large cornmeal cake," he said proudly. "I shall eat it in three bites!"

"My cornmeal cake is larger!" shouted Prince Kojo. "I shall gulp it in two bites!"

Prince Kwame leaned back in his royal chair. "I have eaten three cornmeal cakes already!" he said, laughing at his brothers.

Prince Kijani turned red. "That's not fair!" he cried. "My cornmeal cake is so little."

"Where is my cornmeal cake? It was just here!" Prince Kumi screamed.

In the schoolroom, Prince Kwame couldn't wait to tell his brothers how smart he was. "Watch me!" he said. "I can add any pair of numbers faster than the rest of you."

"I'm the best at art!" Prince Kijani shouted.

"I'm the best writer," Prince Kofi snapped.

"I'm the smartest because I read the most," Prince Kumi said proudly.

This made Prince Kojo angry. "What did you say? I read much more than you!" he roared.

King Dalmar watched his children. "When do they have time to be the best at anything?" he wondered. "They spend all of their time fighting!"

The family gathered in the royal garden for tea. The children yelled all during tea time. Even the birds had to listen to them fight. King Dalmar and Queen Malkia knew they had to do something to stop the fighting.

Queen Malkia whispered something to the king that made him smile. Before sitting down for tea, he called his servant.

"Go out into the grasslands," King Dalmar commanded. "Bring me a bundle of sticks. I have a lesson to teach my sons."

9

The princes stopped everything and went to sit on the steps. They didn't know why their father had sent the servant to collect sticks, but it worried them. They sat quietly, wondering what the lesson would be.

A short while later, the servant returned with the sticks. Then the five sons lined up in front of their father. King Dalmar tied the sticks together with a piece of royal cloth.

"Now," questioned King Dalmar, "which one of you can break this bundle of sticks?"

They all tried to break the bundle, but none of them could do it.

Then the king untied the bundle. He handed each prince a stick.

"Now try to break the stick you have," said King Dalmar.

Snap! Each stick broke easily.

"You are like the sticks," King Dalmar explained. "Together you are much stronger than if you stand alone. Think of all you can do if you work together!"

They knew their father was right. After that the brothers worked together and were much happier.